D0675875

Usborne

Fractions and Decimals

Activity Book

CONTENTS

Check what you've learned with Quick Quizzes at the end of each section. The answers are at the back of the book.

Written by
Rosie Hore

Designed by
Jodie Smith and Sarah Vince

Illustrated by
Luana Rinaldo

Education consultant: Sheila Ebbutt

Fractions

The first section of this book is all about fractions. A fraction just means an equal part or share of something.

Turn to the back of the book to see all the most common fractions together in a 'fraction wall'.

For example, if you shared this cookie equally between two people, they'd get one half each.

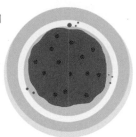

One half is also written like this:

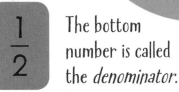

The top number is called the *numerator*.

The bottom number is called the *denominator*.

These are fractions, because they're equal shares.

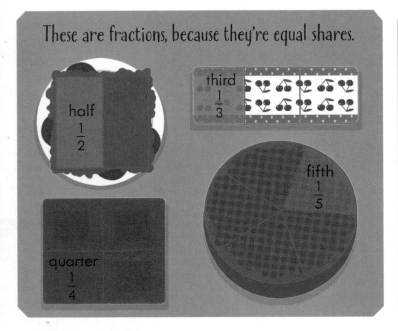

half
$\frac{1}{2}$

third
$\frac{1}{3}$

quarter
$\frac{1}{4}$

fifth
$\frac{1}{5}$

These *aren't* fractions, because the shares *aren't* equal.

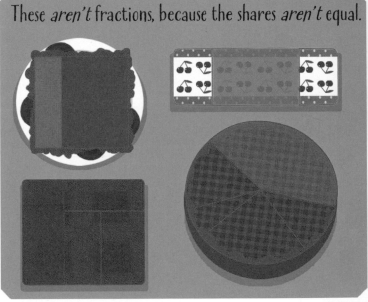

If you cut a pizza into three, and have one slice, that's...

$\frac{1}{3}$

one part...

...out of three parts...

...or one third.

If you have two slices, that's...

$\frac{2}{3}$

two parts...

...out of three parts...

...or two thirds of a pizza.

Using fractions

Fractions are a way of dividing.

For example, to divide 1 chocolate bar between 4...

...you put what you're dividing on top, and the amount you're dividing *by* on the bottom.

 So we all get $\frac{1}{4}$ of the bar!

Sometimes, the result will be more than one.

For example, if you divide 3 cakes between 2 mice...

...each mouse will get three halves...

$\frac{3}{2}$

...which is the same as 1 and a half.

This is called an *improper* fraction. Find out more on page 12.

You can show fractions on a number line, according to their size.

$$0 \quad \frac{1}{10} \quad \frac{1}{5} \quad \frac{1}{4} \quad \frac{1}{3} \quad \frac{1}{2} \quad \frac{2}{3} \quad \frac{3}{4} \quad 1$$

But remember that the *actual* value of a fraction depends on what you had to start with.

What's a half of 10 candy canes?

$\frac{1}{2}$ of $10 = 5$

What's a half of 12 cookies?

$\frac{1}{2}$ of $12 = 6$

$\frac{1}{2}$ of 12 is the same as $\frac{1}{2}$ *multiplied* by 12. Find out more on page 16.

Halves, thirds and quarters

Fractions have to be the same *size*.

I have a whole circle.

I have two halves of a circle.

I *don't* have halves – just two pieces.

But fractions don't have to be the same *shape*.

We've both got a quarter of our sandwich.

Each sandwich is split into 4 equal pieces.

Can you spot a mouse who has eaten a quarter of its cheese, and a mouse who has eaten a half? Circle them both.

A whole cheese looks like this.

These jars were full before the mice got to them. Write the fraction that's *missing* underneath each one.

The actual value of a fraction depends on how much you have to start with.

We shared 4 cookies...

...and half of 4 is 2.

We shared 6 cookies...

...and half of 6 is 3.

The brown mouse eats $\frac{1}{4}$ of the chunks of cheese. Then, the white mouse eats $\frac{1}{3}$ of what's left. Draw a circle around each mouse and the chunks of cheese it eats.

Half of these mice are brown, a third of them are black and the rest are white. Can you fill them in?

Which mouse below is hungrier?

I'm going to eat $\frac{1}{4}$ of these cookies.

I'll munch through $\frac{1}{3}$ of these.

How many shares?

The numerator (the number on top) tells you how many shares you have.

$\frac{1}{3}$

The numerator is one, so you have one third.

$\frac{2}{3}$

A two means you've got two thirds.

$\frac{3}{3}$

Three thirds make a whole.

Draw a line between each customer and their ice cream.

Three customers are sharing two ice creams between them. How much will they get each?

Circle the answer.

$\frac{1}{2}$ $\frac{3}{4}$ $\frac{2}{3}$

Mine is half strawberry and half chocolate.

Mine is three fifths vanilla.

Mine is two thirds mint.

There's been an order for ten ice cream sundaes. Can you answer the questions underneath?

Of the sundaes, what fraction has sprinkles? $\frac{2}{10}$

What fraction has pink ice cream? $\frac{3}{10}$

What fraction has orange ice cream? $\frac{1}{10}$

What fraction has strawberries? $\frac{5}{10}$

Make the ice cream cakes according to the recipes, using the stickers on the sticker pages.

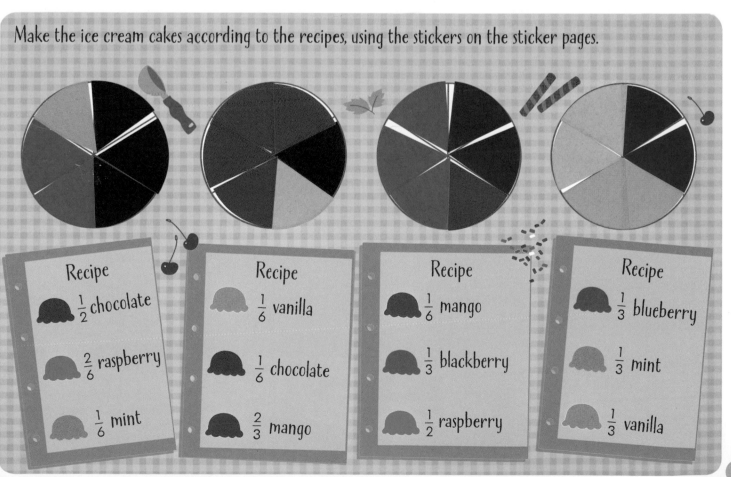

Recipe
$\frac{1}{2}$ chocolate
$\frac{2}{6}$ raspberry
$\frac{1}{6}$ mint

Recipe
$\frac{1}{6}$ vanilla
$\frac{1}{6}$ chocolate
$\frac{2}{3}$ mango

Recipe
$\frac{1}{6}$ mango
$\frac{1}{3}$ blackberry
$\frac{1}{2}$ raspberry

Recipe
$\frac{1}{3}$ blueberry
$\frac{1}{3}$ mint
$\frac{1}{3}$ vanilla

Equivalent fractions

Fractions with the same value are called *equivalent* fractions.

For example...

$$\frac{1}{2} = \frac{2}{4} = \frac{4}{8}$$

$$\frac{1}{3} = \frac{2}{6} = \frac{4}{12}$$

You'll find a bigger fraction wall on the last page of the book.

$\frac{1}{2}$				$\frac{1}{2}$			
$\frac{1}{4}$		$\frac{1}{4}$		$\frac{1}{4}$		$\frac{1}{4}$	
$\frac{1}{8}$	$\frac{1}{8}$	$\frac{1}{8}$	$\frac{1}{8}$	$\frac{1}{8}$	$\frac{1}{8}$	$\frac{1}{8}$	$\frac{1}{8}$

You can find equivalent fractions using fraction walls, like these.

$\frac{1}{3}$				$\frac{1}{3}$				$\frac{1}{3}$			
$\frac{1}{6}$		$\frac{1}{6}$		$\frac{1}{6}$		$\frac{1}{6}$		$\frac{1}{6}$		$\frac{1}{6}$	
$\frac{1}{12}$	$\frac{1}{12}$	$\frac{1}{12}$	$\frac{1}{12}$	$\frac{1}{12}$	$\frac{1}{12}$	$\frac{1}{12}$	$\frac{1}{12}$	$\frac{1}{12}$	$\frac{1}{12}$	$\frac{1}{12}$	$\frac{1}{12}$

Join each owl to the baby owl with the equivalent fraction.

Help this squirrel arrange his acorns from smallest to largest, using the stickers from the sticker pages.

Three of the fractions on each branch are equivalent. Can you circle the ones that *aren't* the same?

$\frac{8}{12}$　$\frac{4}{6}$　$\frac{3}{4}$　$\frac{2}{3}$

$\frac{2}{4}$　$\frac{4}{8}$

$\frac{1}{4}$　$\frac{1}{2}$　$\frac{2}{6}$　$\frac{4}{12}$

$\frac{1}{3}$　$\frac{3}{8}$

Can you add spots to the eggs in the nests?

$\frac{1}{3}$ of these eggs need spots.

$\frac{1}{2}$ of these eggs need spots.

$\frac{3}{4}$ of these eggs need spots.

$\frac{2}{3}$ of these eggs need spots.

$$\frac{1}{3} = \frac{2}{6}$$

$$\frac{1}{2} = \frac{2}{4}$$

$$\frac{3}{4} = \frac{6}{8}$$

$$\frac{2}{3} = \frac{4}{6}$$

Help the baby bird find the nest with the right fraction, using her clue.

The fraction is bigger than $\frac{1}{4}$, but smaller than $\frac{3}{4}$.

Use the fraction wall to see how they compare.

$\frac{1}{8}$　$\frac{3}{8}$　$\frac{7}{8}$　$\frac{6}{8}$

Simplifying fractions

Simplifying a fraction means converting it into an equivalent fraction with a smaller denominator (bottom).

To do this, you divide the top and the bottom by the same number.

For example:

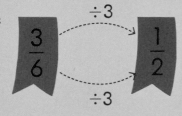

$$\frac{3}{6} \xrightarrow{\div 3}{}_{\div 3} \frac{1}{2}$$

It can be easier to simplify in stages.

$$\frac{8}{24} \xrightarrow{\div 2}{}_{\div 2} \frac{4}{12} \xrightarrow{\div 4}{}_{\div 4} \frac{1}{3}$$

Keep going until you can't divide the top and bottom by the same number any more.

Circle the fractions that can't be simplified any further.

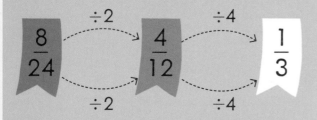

$\frac{6}{8}$

$\frac{6}{13}$

$\frac{4}{16}$

$\frac{4}{7}$

$\frac{6}{10}$

Simplify the fractions on the kennels, then match them up with the dogs.

Simplify the fractions on the dog treats by dividing the top and the bottom by the same number.

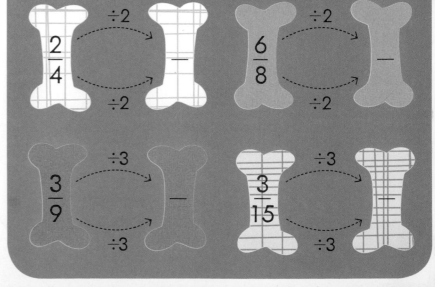

$$\frac{2}{4} \xrightarrow{\div 2}{}_{\div 2} \underline{}$$

$$\frac{6}{8} \xrightarrow{\div 2}{}_{\div 2} \underline{}$$

$$\frac{3}{9} \xrightarrow{\div 3}{}_{\div 3} \underline{}$$

$$\frac{3}{15} \xrightarrow{\div 3}{}_{\div 3} \underline{}$$

Six dogs have had their photographs taken. Can you answer the questions below?
Don't forget to simplify your answers.

🐾 Of all the dogs, what fraction has a collar?

$$\frac{4}{6} = \frac{2}{3}$$

🐾 Of the collars, what fraction is pink?

$$\frac{3}{4} = \frac{3}{4}$$

🐾 Of all the dogs, what fraction has bows?

$$\frac{3}{6} = \frac{1}{2}$$

🐾 Of the bows, what fraction is yellow?

$$\frac{6}{9} = \frac{2}{3}$$

It's time to announce the results of a dog show! Simplify the fractions on the banner, then match the simplified fractions with the fractions below the dogs, adding in the letters to spell out their names.

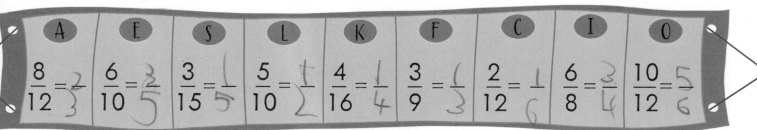

A	E	S	L	K	F	C	I	O
$\frac{8}{12}=\frac{2}{3}$	$\frac{6}{10}=\frac{3}{5}$	$\frac{3}{15}=\frac{1}{5}$	$\frac{5}{10}=\frac{1}{2}$	$\frac{4}{16}=\frac{1}{4}$	$\frac{3}{9}=\frac{1}{3}$	$\frac{2}{12}=\frac{1}{6}$	$\frac{6}{8}=\frac{3}{4}$	$\frac{10}{12}=\frac{5}{6}$

P L A C K
$\frac{1}{3}$ $\frac{1}{2}$ $\frac{3}{4}$ $\frac{1}{6}$ $\frac{1}{4}$

S O C K S
$\frac{1}{5}$ $\frac{5}{6}$ $\frac{1}{6}$ $\frac{1}{4}$ $\frac{1}{5}$

A L F I E
$\frac{2}{3}$ $\frac{1}{2}$ $\frac{1}{3}$ $\frac{3}{4}$ $\frac{3}{5}$

Proper, improper and mixed fractions

This is a *proper* fraction. $\frac{3}{4}$

The numerator is smaller than the denominator.

This is an *improper* fraction. $\frac{5}{4}$

The numerator is *bigger* than the denominator.

You can convert an improper fraction into a *mixed* fraction, like this.

$$\frac{5}{4} = 1\frac{1}{4}$$

Four quarters make a whole, so $\frac{5}{4}$ is one whole plus one quarter.

These knights are battling a fierce dragon. Finish the dragon using the clues.

- All the *proper* fractions are red.
- All the *improper* fractions are yellow.
- All the *mixed* fractions are green.

$2\frac{1}{10}$

$1\frac{1}{6}$

$1\frac{7}{10}$

$1\frac{1}{5}$

$1\frac{2}{3}$

$2\frac{1}{2}$

$\frac{9}{4}$

$\frac{8}{5}$

$\frac{5}{10}$

$1\frac{4}{6}$

$\frac{2}{10}$

$\frac{3}{2}$

$\frac{5}{6}$

$\frac{5}{2}$

$\frac{8}{6}$

$\frac{4}{3}$

$\frac{8}{5}$

The knight with the biggest number defeated the dragon. Convert the fractions to find out which one it was.

$\frac{11}{10}$

$\frac{15}{5}$

$\frac{5}{2}$

The knights are making their way back to the castle. Can you convert the improper fractions into mixed fractions, to find their route?

Pass the fractions in this order...
$\frac{8}{5}$ $\frac{7}{4}$ $\frac{10}{9}$ $\frac{5}{2}$ $\frac{5}{3}$ $\frac{9}{4}$

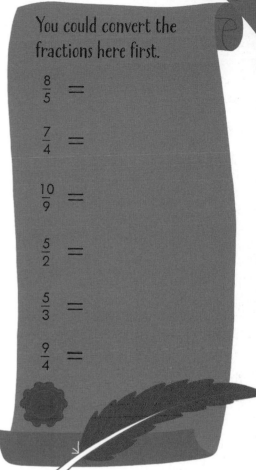

You could convert the fractions here first.

$\frac{8}{5}$ =

$\frac{7}{4}$ =

$\frac{10}{9}$ =

$\frac{5}{2}$ =

$\frac{5}{3}$ =

$\frac{9}{4}$ =

Map labels:
$1\frac{3}{5}$ $1\frac{3}{4}$ $2\frac{1}{12}$
$2\frac{3}{5}$ $1\frac{1}{9}$ $1\frac{1}{3}$
$2\frac{1}{5}$ $2\frac{3}{10}$
$1\frac{1}{2}$
$1\frac{1}{5}$ $2\frac{1}{2}$
$2\frac{1}{3}$ $1\frac{1}{8}$
$2\frac{3}{5}$
$1\frac{2}{3}$ $1\frac{1}{5}$
$1\frac{1}{4}$ $2\frac{1}{4}$

It's time for a feast. Are there enough pies for all the knights to have the amount they want?   YES / NO
Hint: Try drawing thirds on the pies first.

I'll eat $\frac{5}{3}$ of a pie!

Give me $\frac{2}{3}$ of a pie!

I want $1\frac{1}{3}$ pies!

Using fractions to divide

Fractions are a way of sharing or dividing.

For example, to divide 2 jars of treats between 5 party bags...

...you put the number of things you're dividing on top...

$\dfrac{2}{5}$

...and the number you're dividing *by* on the bottom.

So each party bag will have $\frac{2}{5}$ of a jar.

If you divided 3 birthday cakes between 4 plates, what fraction of 1 cake would be on each plate? Show your answer with stickers from the sticker pages.

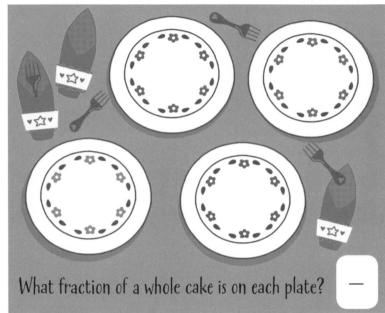

What fraction of a whole cake is on each plate? ☐—

Share 2 pineapple pizzas between 3 guests.

Share 4 pepperoni pizzas between 7 guests.

Share 5 mushroom pizzas between 6 guests.

Each person gets ☐— of a pizza.　Each person gets ☐— of a pizza.　Each person gets ☐— of a pizza.

Answer these questions to share out the party food. Remember to simplify your answers.

Divide 4 cartons of juice between 6 cups. What fraction of a carton will be in each cup?

Share 4 cartons of popcorn between 8 bowls. What fraction of a carton will be in each bowl?

Share 3 slices of melons between 6 plates. What fraction of a slice will be on each plate?

$$\frac{4}{6} = \frac{}{3}$$

$$\frac{}{} = \frac{}{}$$

$$\frac{}{} = \frac{}{}$$

Add a balloon from the sticker pages to each string. Answer the division questions using fractions, then simplify your answers to find which balloon goes where.

$5 \div 2$ $\qquad$ $6 \div 9$ $\qquad$ $8 \div 5$ $\qquad$ $2 \div 4$ $\qquad$ $3 \div 9$ $\qquad$ $4 \div 10$ $\qquad$ $10 \div 3$

Finding a fraction of a number

Finding $\frac{1}{2}$ of a number is the same as dividing by 2.

$$\frac{1}{2} \text{ of } 8 = 4$$

Finding $\frac{1}{3}$ of a number is the same as dividing by 3.

$$\frac{1}{3} \text{ of } 9 = 3$$

You always *divide* by the *denominator*. So...

$$\frac{1}{7} \text{ of } 14 = 14 \div 7 = 2$$

You can also write the 'of' as times or 'x'. $\frac{1}{2}$ of 4 is the same as $\frac{1}{2}$ times 4.

These robots are finding fractions of numbers. Write the number each one should divide by on the dotted line, then write the answer in the white circle. The first one has been done for you.

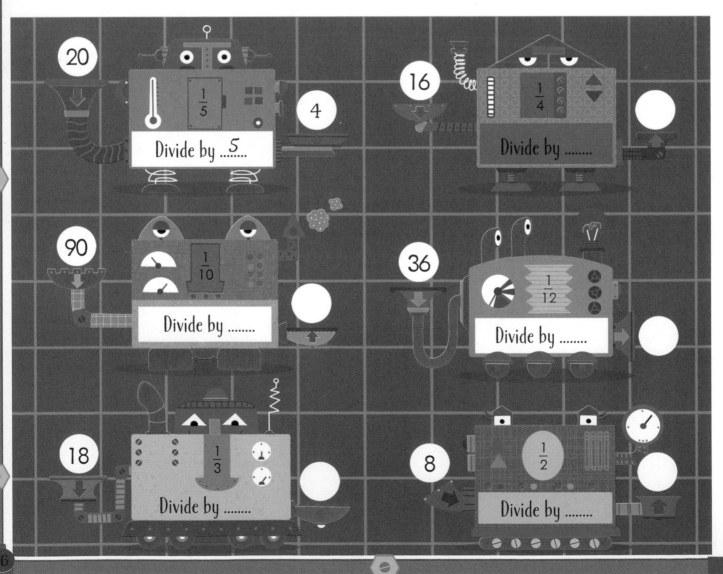

20 — $\frac{1}{5}$ — Divide by ...5... — 4

16 — $\frac{1}{4}$ — Divide by ....

90 — $\frac{1}{10}$ — Divide by ....

36 — $\frac{1}{12}$ — Divide by ....

18 — $\frac{1}{3}$ — Divide by ....

8 — $\frac{1}{2}$ — Divide by ....

It's a busy day at the robot factory. Can you work out how many boxes each robot has delivered? Give the robot that has delivered the most boxes a sticker from the sticker pages.

This robot is packing a box full of spare parts. Can you find his route around the factory, picking up parts on the way? Follow the order shown on the right.

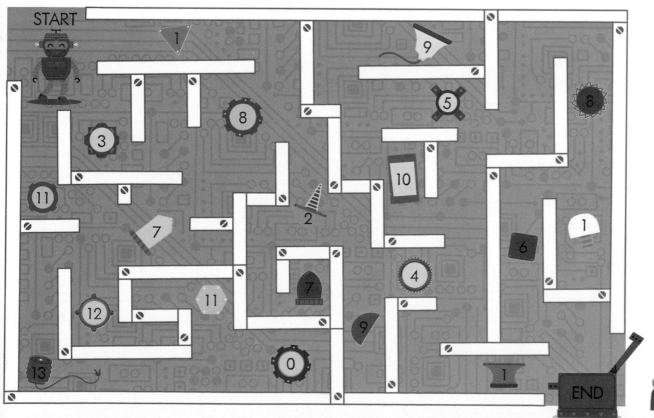

$\frac{1}{4}$ of 12

$\frac{1}{5}$ of 40

$\frac{1}{8}$ of 16

$\frac{1}{6}$ of 24

$\frac{1}{10}$ of 100

$\frac{1}{5}$ of 25

$\frac{1}{3}$ of 24

$\frac{1}{2}$ of 12

Finding more fractions

To find a fraction of a number when the numerator is more than one, you *divide* by the denominator, then *multiply* the result by the numerator.

For example...

I spent $\frac{2}{3}$ of my 15 coins at the last port.

How many coins did she spend?

Divide by the denominator (bottom) to find one third.

$$15 \div 3 = 5$$

Multiply the result by the numerator (top) to find two thirds.

$$5 \times 2 = 10 \text{ coins}$$

Try it yourself here...

What's $\frac{3}{10}$ of 60 gold coins?

First, find a tenth.

$$60 \div$$

Then multiply your answer by the numerator to find three tenths.

The chest with the biggest answer contains the most treasure. Can you work out which one it is? Add a sticker to it once you've found it.

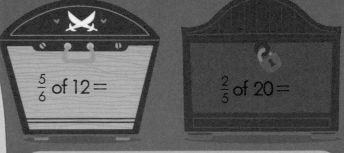

$\frac{5}{6}$ of 12 =

$\frac{2}{5}$ of 20 =

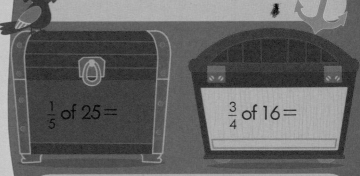

$\frac{1}{5}$ of 25 =

$\frac{3}{4}$ of 16 =

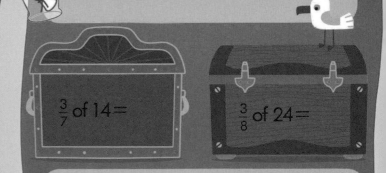

$\frac{3}{7}$ of 14 =

$\frac{3}{8}$ of 24 =

Use the key to finish this treasure map with stickers from the sticker pages. Stick the sticker in the square with the correct number, then find a route from the pirate ship sticker to the X sticker, avoiding whirlpools and sharks.

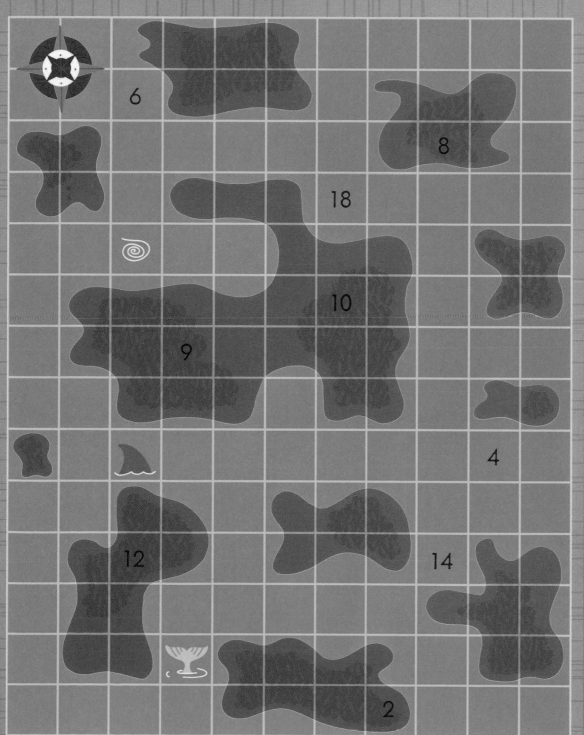

$\frac{9}{10}$ of 20

$\frac{2}{3}$ of 9

$\frac{3}{10}$ of 40

$\frac{3}{4}$ of 12

$\frac{2}{5}$ of 10

$\frac{7}{8}$ of 16

$\frac{5}{6}$ of 12

$\frac{2}{9}$ of 9

$\frac{4}{5}$ of 10

Use this space for working.

Comparing fractions

It's easier to compare fractions if they have a shared or *common* denominator.

For example...

What's bigger: $\frac{2}{3}$ or $\frac{3}{5}$?

To find the common denominator, multiply together the two denominators you started with.

$$3 \times 5 = 15$$

That tells you that both fractions can be converted into fifteenths.

This is how you do it...

For $\frac{2}{3}$, multiply the top and the bottom by 5.

For $\frac{3}{5}$, you multiply the top and bottom by 3.

So $\frac{2}{3}$ is bigger than $\frac{3}{5}$.

Circle the best deal on this market stall. (You're looking for the biggest fraction.) The common denominator is 15 (5x3).

T-SHIRTS $\frac{2}{3}$ off!

SCARVES $\frac{4}{5}$ off!

$\frac{2}{3} \overset{\times 5}{\underset{\times 5}{=}} \overline{15}$

$\frac{4}{5} \overset{\times 3}{\underset{\times 3}{=}} \overline{15}$

What about this stall? Find the common denominator by multiplying the two denominators together.

BAGS $\frac{1}{2}$ off!

DRESSES $\frac{4}{7}$ off!

$\frac{1}{2} \overset{\times}{\underset{\times}{=}} \overline{}$

$\frac{4}{7} \overset{\times}{\underset{\times}{=}} \overline{}$

Which stall has sold the biggest fraction?

I've sold $\frac{3}{5}$ of my hats.

I've sold $\frac{3}{4}$ of my watches.

Use this space for any working out.

Follow the clues below to decorate the shoppers' bags. You can convert the fractions in your head, or use the space below.

The bag with the smallest fraction has stripes.

The bag with the biggest fraction has spots.

The bag with zigzags has a bigger fraction than the bag with flowers.

$\frac{2}{3}$

$\frac{1}{2}$

$\frac{5}{6}$

$\frac{1}{6}$

Adding and subtracting fractions

When fractions have matching denominators, you can add or subtract the numerators like this.

$$\frac{3}{7} + \frac{2}{7} = \frac{5}{7}$$

$$\frac{5}{9} - \frac{3}{9} = \frac{2}{9}$$

If the denominators *don't* match...

What's $\frac{3}{4}$ plus $\frac{2}{3}$?

...you need to convert the fractions so that they do...

$$\frac{3}{4} \overset{\times 3}{\underset{\times 3}{=}} \frac{9}{12} \qquad \frac{2}{3} \overset{\times 4}{\underset{\times 4}{=}} \frac{8}{12}$$

...before you add.

$$\frac{9}{12} + \frac{8}{12} = \frac{17}{12} = 1\frac{5}{12}$$

The big goat eats two thirds of the food in the trough and the kid eats a sixth. How much is that altogether?
(Hint: Convert the first fraction into sixths.)

$$\frac{2}{3} + \frac{1}{6} =$$

Follow the clues to put the horses from the sticker pages into their stalls in the stable.

The sum on the white horse's stall equals 1.
The sum on the brown horse's stall equals $\frac{1}{2}$.
The sum on the black horse's stall equals $1\frac{1}{2}$.

Use this space for working.

$$\frac{1}{3} + \frac{1}{6}$$

$$\frac{2}{3} + \frac{5}{6}$$

$$\frac{3}{7} + \frac{4}{7}$$

Can you find the sum of all the fractions on the sheep?

$\frac{1}{8}$

$\frac{1}{2}$

$\frac{1}{4}$

$\frac{5}{8}$

$\frac{1}{4}$

$\frac{3}{8}$

$\frac{3}{4}$

$\frac{1}{8}$

It's feeding time at the farm. Can you work out how many bags of seed the birds eat in total?

- Each chicken eats $\frac{1}{4}$ of a bag of seed.
- Each chick eats *half* as much as a chicken.
- Each rooster eats *twice* as much as a chicken.

Use this space for working.

bags of seed

23

Each monkey had 6 bananas to begin with. What fraction does each one have left? Use this space for your working out, and remember to simplify your answers.

Add poison dart frogs from the sticker pages to these leaves. $\frac{2}{5}$ of the leaves have green frogs on them, and $\frac{3}{10}$ of the leaves have red frogs.

Three toucans are sharing eight mangoes equally. What fraction will they get each?

Figure out the calculations below, then stick the butterfly sticker with the correct answer on top.

$\frac{1}{2}$ of 12

$\frac{3}{7}$ of 21

$\frac{5}{6}$ of 18

$\frac{4}{7}$ of 14

$\frac{1}{5}$ of 15

$\frac{3}{4}$ of 16

Shade the snakes' bodies following the fractions.

$\frac{1}{3}$ yellow
$\frac{2}{3}$ blue

$\frac{1}{4}$ purple
$\frac{5}{8}$ green
$\frac{1}{8}$ yellow

$\frac{1}{3}$ yellow
$\frac{2}{9}$ red
$\frac{4}{9}$ green

25

What fraction of each shape is shaded?
Write your answers in the boxes.

  $\frac{2}{3}$ $\frac{3}{8}$

 $\frac{7}{0}$ $\frac{2}{5}$

  $\frac{3}{4}$ $\frac{5}{10}$

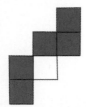  $\frac{5}{6}$  $\frac{1}{7}$

Check your answers at
the back of the book,
then choose a star from
the sticker pages.

Score
$\frac{7}{8}$

Sticker

Simplify these fractions.

$\frac{3}{12} = \frac{1}{4}$

$\frac{4}{10} = \frac{2}{5}$

$\frac{3}{6} = \frac{1}{2}$

$\frac{14}{20} = \frac{7}{10}$

Convert these improper
fractions into mixed fractions.

$\frac{7}{4} =$

$\frac{10}{3} =$

$\frac{17}{8} =$

Score
$\frac{}{7}$

Sticker

26

Find the value of these fractions.

$\frac{2}{3}$ of 15 =

$\frac{3}{4}$ of 12 =

$\frac{3}{10}$ of 30 =

$\frac{4}{7}$ of 21 =

$\frac{5}{6}$ of 18 =

$\frac{1}{4}$ of 20 =

Score

$\frac{}{6}$

Sticker

Find the answers to these fraction questions, and simplify your answers.

$\frac{2}{3} + \frac{2}{3} =$

$\frac{1}{3} - \frac{1}{6} =$

$\frac{4}{5} - \frac{3}{10} =$

$\frac{1}{12} + \frac{2}{6} =$

$\frac{3}{5} + \frac{2}{10} =$

$\frac{1}{3} - \frac{1}{4} =$

Score

$\frac{}{6}$

Sticker

Decimals

This section of the book is all about decimals. Decimals are another way of writing fractions out of 10, 100 or 1,000 (or other tens of tens), like this...

$\frac{1}{10}$ → 0.1

$\frac{1}{100}$ → 0.01

$\frac{1}{1000}$ → 0.001

Decimals are written using *place value*, which means that *where* a number goes tells you how much it's worth.

| Hundreds | Tens | Ones | | Tenths | Hundredths | Thousandths |

2 6 5 . 7 1 5

The numbers on this side are *whole* numbers.

Decimal point

The numbers on this side are decimal fractions.

The places after the decimal point are known as *decimal places*.

Look for place value to see how much each number is worth.

This is worth 7 ones. **7.9** This is worth 9 tenths.

This is worth 1 ten. **10.03** This is worth 3 hundredths.

Zero is used as a *place holder*, to show when there's nothing there.

0.3
A zero *before* a decimal point shows there are no ones.

4.02
A zero here shows there are no tenths.

4.2⊘
You *don't* need a zero at the end if there's nothing after it.

Converting decimals

When you're converting fractions into decimals — and the other way around — it helps to remember how many decimal places you'll need.

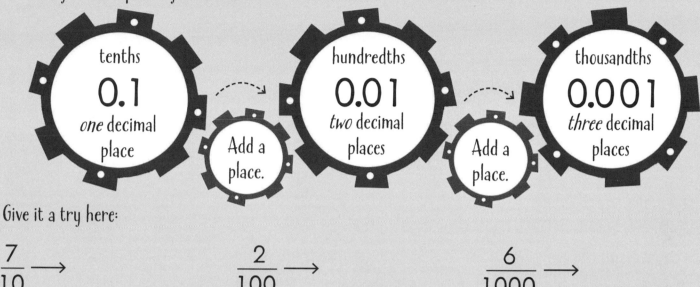

tenths
0.1
one decimal place

Add a place.

hundredths
0.01
two decimal places

Add a place.

thousandths
0.001
three decimal places

Give it a try here:

$$\frac{7}{10} \longrightarrow$$

$$\frac{2}{100} \longrightarrow$$

$$\frac{6}{1000} \longrightarrow$$

Number lines

On a number line, decimals come between the whole numbers. Can you fill in the gaps?

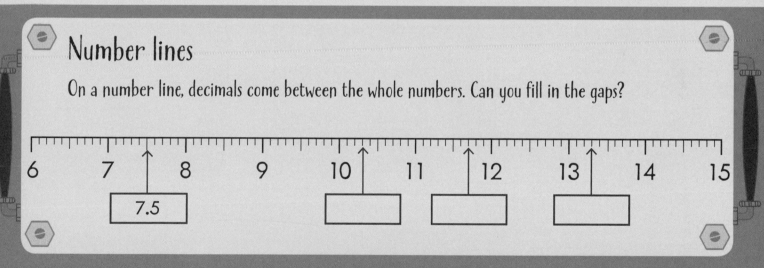

6   7   8   9   10   11   12   13   14   15

7.5

Some decimals may be more precise than you need. Finding the nearest whole number or the nearest tenth can make the numbers easier to handle. This is called *rounding*.

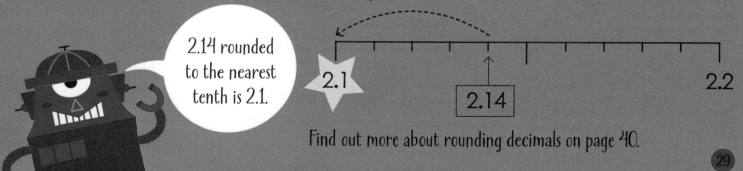

2.14 rounded to the nearest tenth is 2.1.

2.1

2.14

2.2

Find out more about rounding decimals on page 40.

Tenths

When you're converting fractions into decimals, remember to think about place value. Try these fractions with tenths first.

$\dfrac{8}{10} =$ ☐ **.** ☐   Ones   Tenths

$2\dfrac{3}{10} =$ ☐ **.** ☐   Ones   Tenths

$7\dfrac{7}{10} =$ ☐ **.** ☐   Ones   Tenths

There are ten cars waiting at the traffic lights. Can you answer the questions below, and then convert your fractions into decimals?

Of all the cars, what fraction is red?

☐   ☐
Fraction   Decimal

Of all the cars, what fraction has an open top?

☐   ☐
Fraction   Decimal

Of all the cars, what fraction is blue?

☐   ☐
Fraction   Decimal

Park the cars from the sticker pages, following the taken spaces sign.

Which space is left for me?

0.7	0.9	1.1	0.4
2.1	1.2	0.2	0.5

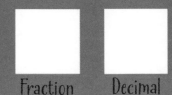

TAKEN SPACES

$\dfrac{9}{10}$ $\dfrac{5}{10}$ $\dfrac{4}{10}$

$1\dfrac{1}{10}$ $\dfrac{7}{10}$

$1\dfrac{2}{10}$ $2\dfrac{1}{10}$

Hundredths

Can you convert these fractions with hundredths into decimals?

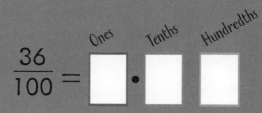

$\dfrac{4}{100}$ = [Ones] • [Tenths] [Hundredths]

If there are no tenths, put a 0 in the tenths column.

$\dfrac{36}{100}$ = [Ones] • [Tenths] [Hundredths]

(36 hundredths is the same as 3 tenths and 6 hundredths.)

Remember that hundredths need two decimal places.

Fill in the picture, matching the decimals to the fractions below to find the correct shades.

$\dfrac{1}{100}$ $\dfrac{5}{100}$

$\dfrac{15}{100}$ $\dfrac{25}{100}$

$\dfrac{50}{100}$ $\dfrac{75}{100}$

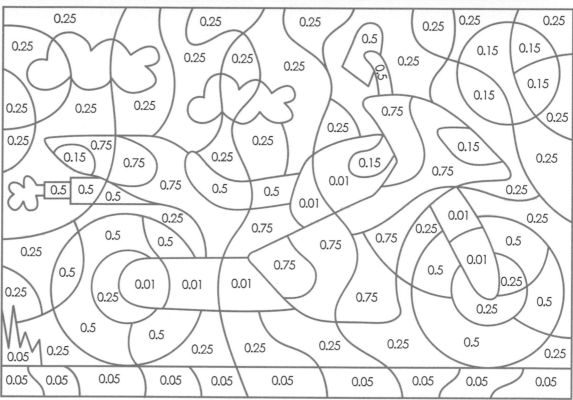

These cars are waiting to fill up. They'll go in order, from the smallest number to the biggest number. Can you work out the order, then write 1st, 2nd, 3rd, 4th and 5th next to the cars?

0.3   0.6   3.6 $\dfrac{36}{100}$ $\dfrac{6}{100}$

31

Decimal measurements

Decimals are useful when you're measuring in metric.

Length

There are 10 millimetres (mm) in a centimetre (cm) and 100 cm in a metre (m).

10 mm = 1 cm
1 mm = 0.1 cm

100 cm = 1 m
10 cm = 0.1 m
1 cm = 0.01 m

CHOC DREAM

This chocolate is 5.4 cm long (which is the same as 5 cm and 4 mm).

0 1 2 3 4 5 6 7 8 9

Each of the small lines on the ruler is 1 mm, or 0.1 cm.

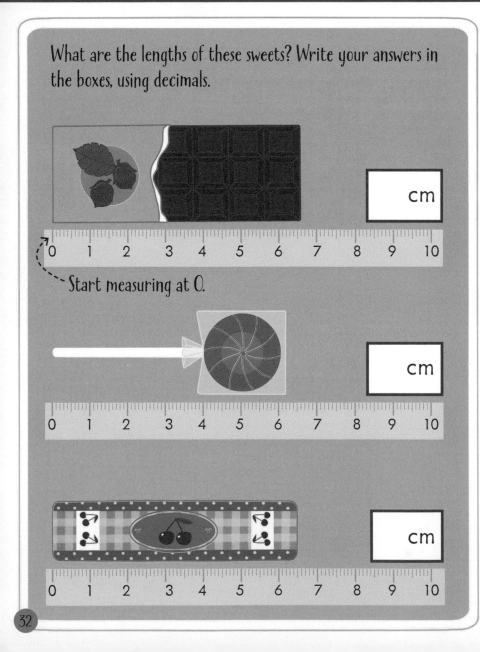

What are the lengths of these sweets? Write your answers in the boxes, using decimals.

cm

0 1 2 3 4 5 6 7 8 9 10

Start measuring at 0.

cm

0 1 2 3 4 5 6 7 8 9 10

cm

0 1 2 3 4 5 6 7 8 9 10

Circle the bag of flour this customer should buy.

My recipe needs 1,200 g of flour.

0.2 kg

1 kg

1.2 kg

Mass

There are 1,000 grams (g) in a kilogram (kg).

1,000 g = 1 kg
100 g = 0.1 kg
10 g = 0.01 kg
1 g = 0.001 kg

This bag of potatoes weighs 900 g, or 0.9 kg.

Volume

There are 1,000 millilitres (ml) in a litre (l).

1,000 ml = 1 l
100 ml = 0.1 l
10 ml = 0.01 l
1 ml = 0.001 l

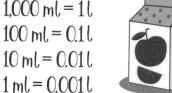

This carton of juice contains 500 ml, or 0.5 l.

Find the items on the shelves that match the shopping list exactly. Circle them.

300 g bag of cherries

0.4 kg box of cereal

200 ml bottle of milk

750 ml carton of juice

400 g bag of grapes

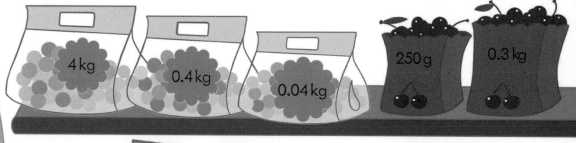

Circle the product in each pair which has *more*.

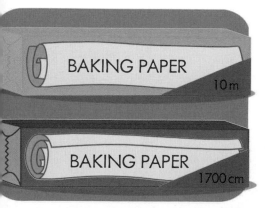

BAKING PAPER 10 m

BAKING PAPER 1700 cm

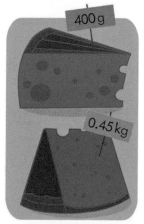

400 g

0.45 kg

450 ml

0.5 l

0.08 kg

70 g

Decimal money

Many types of money, including pounds (£), dollars ($) and euros (€), use decimal places.

Whole pounds, (or dollars or euros) go on this side.

decimal point

£14.05

Pennies or cents go on this side. (A hundred pennies make a pound, so each penny is 0.01 pounds.)

Money is always written with two decimal places, even if there's nothing after the decimal point.

£14.00

Join up the pair of items that you could buy for exactly £1.00. Then join the pairs you could buy for exactly £2.00, for exactly £3.00 and for exactly £4.00.

£0.86   £0.14   £1.99   £0.75

£1.25   £1.66   £1.34   £2.01

How much will everything cost?

€15.55   €1.23   €0.77   €2.45

TOTAL

€

Will I get any change from a €20.00 note?

YES / NO

Look out for pairs which add up to whole euros.

Some of the numbers are missing on these receipts. Can you fill in the blanks?
Count on from the first price until you get to the total.

light bulb	£4.50
lampshade	_____
TOTAL	£11.00

tap	$15.00
mop	_____
TOTAL	$20.60

wood glue	€2.40
planks	_____
TOTAL	€12.60

What are the new prices? Fill in the labels.

SUPER SUMMER SALE!

Everything HALF price.

WAS $4.50 NOW $

WAS $3.20 NOW $

WAS $5.00 NOW $

How much will each person pay?

Pink paint
£0.50 per 100 ml

Blackboard paint
£0.60 per 100 ml

Glow in the dark paint
£1.20 per 100 ml

£........

£........

£........

I need 500 ml of pink paint for my bedroom door.

I need 0.5l of blackboard paint for my kitchen wall.

I'm buying 0.2l of paint to make my bike glow in the dark.

Remember, there are 1,000 ml in a litre.

More conversions

When you're converting fractions into decimals, you might need to convert the fraction into tenths or hundredths first.

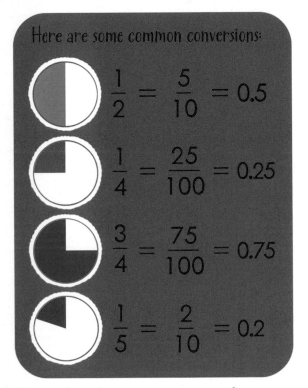

Here are some common conversions:

$$\frac{1}{2} = \frac{5}{10} = 0.5$$

$$\frac{1}{4} = \frac{25}{100} = 0.25$$

$$\frac{3}{4} = \frac{75}{100} = 0.75$$

$$\frac{1}{5} = \frac{2}{10} = 0.2$$

Remember, fractions are a way of dividing. So you can also convert fractions into decimals by dividing, either in your head or on a calculator.

$$\frac{1}{8} = 1 \div 8 = 0.125$$

Sometimes, the answer won't be exact. For example...

$$\frac{1}{3} = 1 \div 3 = 0.333333333...$$

Here, the threes go on forever. This is known as 0.3 recurring, or $0.\dot{3}$.

Shade in each snowball, to show the decimal beneath.

0.25

0.75

0.5

0.6

0.2

0.8

Choose four fish from the sticker pages that have decimals of the same value as the fractions on these seals, and stick them down.

$\frac{1}{4}$

$\frac{4}{5}$

$\frac{1}{5}$

$\frac{1}{2}$

The egg that is *different* from the other two in each group will hatch first. Can you find it and stick a baby penguin from the sticker pages on top?

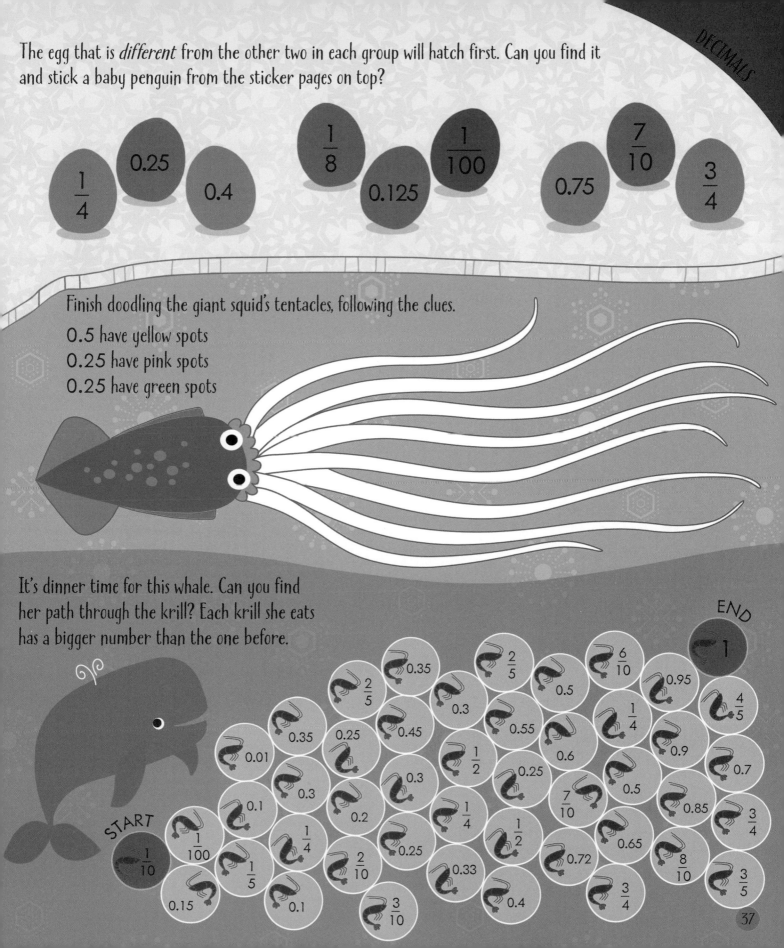

$\frac{1}{4}$ 0.25   0.4

$\frac{1}{8}$ 0.125 $\frac{1}{100}$

0.75 $\frac{7}{10}$ $\frac{3}{4}$

Finish doodling the giant squid's tentacles, following the clues.

0.5 have yellow spots
0.25 have pink spots
0.25 have green spots

It's dinner time for this whale. Can you find her path through the krill? Each krill she eats has a bigger number than the one before.

END
1

START
$\frac{1}{10}$

0.35 $\frac{2}{5}$ $\frac{6}{10}$ 0.95

$\frac{2}{5}$ 0.3   0.5 $\frac{1}{4}$ $\frac{4}{5}$

0.35   0.25   0.45   0.55   0.9   0.7

0.01   0.3 $\frac{1}{2}$ 0.6   0.5   0.85 $\frac{3}{4}$

0.1   0.2 $\frac{1}{4}$ 0.25 $\frac{7}{10}$ 0.65 $\frac{8}{10}$ $\frac{3}{5}$

$\frac{1}{100}$ $\frac{1}{4}$ 0.25 $\frac{1}{4}$ $\frac{1}{2}$ 0.72 $\frac{3}{4}$

0.15 $\frac{1}{5}$ 0.1 $\frac{2}{10}$ 0.33   0.4

$\frac{3}{10}$

Finding a decimal of a number

To find 0.1 of a number, you need to divide it by 10.

$$0.1 \text{ of } 30 = 30 \div 10 = 3$$

What about 0.4 of 20? Find 0.1 and then multiply it by 4.

Divide 20 by 10 to find 0.1...

$$20 \div 10 = 2$$

...then multiply your answer by 4.

$$2 \times 4 = 8$$

So 0.4 of 20 = 8.

In some cases, it could be quicker to think of the fraction you're working out.

$$0.25 = \frac{1}{4} \quad 0.5 = \frac{1}{2} \quad 0.75 = \frac{3}{4}$$

You can also use a calculator. Remember that 'of' means the same as 'multiply' or 'times' (x).

So to find 0.3 of 20, you put in...

$$0.3 \times 20$$

...to get the answer (it's 6).

One of these containers contains a golden ticket. Can you find it, using the clues below? Add a sticker to the right one.

It's even. It's more than 10. It's less than 15.

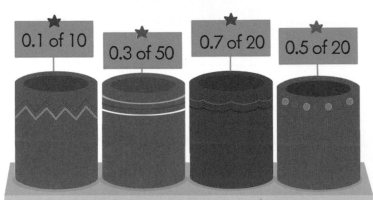

0.1 of 10   0.3 of 50   0.7 of 20   0.5 of 20

Use this space for working out.

Can you find the winning card? Start by crossing out any pairs of cards that show the same answer – the winner is the one left.

0.4 of 40

0.1 of 40

0.5 of 24

0.2 of 20

0.5 of 32

In this game, you multiply the number on the dart by the decimal it hits to find out your points. How many points have these darts won altogether?

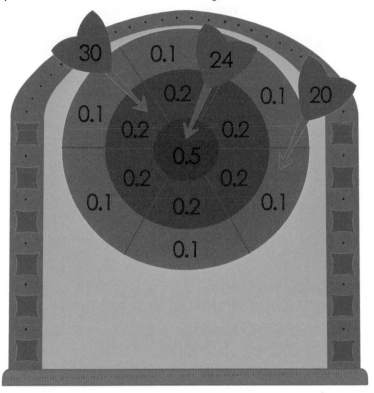

If you start with 5 balls, how many go in each basket, according to the signs? Use stickers to show your answer.

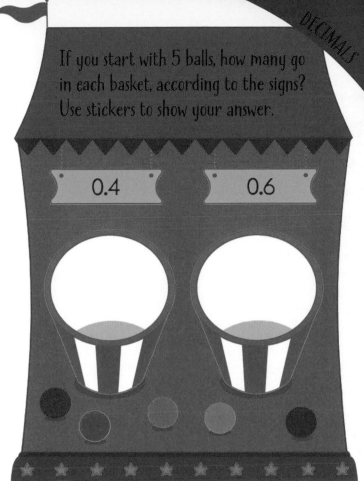

Work out the decimals below, then join the answers with straight lines to show the route of the bumper car. You can work them out in your head, or use a calculator.

0.2 of 20 =

0.5 of 50 =

0.75 of 4 =

0.3 of 20 =

0.7 of 10 =

0.5 of 26 =

0.25 of 20 =

How many cars will I bump?

Start here.

Rounding decimals

To round to the nearest *whole* number, look at the number in the tenths column.

If it's 5 or more, you round up.

$$3.5 \longrightarrow 4$$

If it's 4 or less, you round down.

$$6.4 \longrightarrow 6$$

It doesn't matter if there are any hundredths or not.

$$8.49 \longrightarrow 8$$

If you're rounding to the nearest *tenth*, look at the number in the hundredths column.

If it's 5 or more, you round up.

$$7.36 \longrightarrow 7.4$$

If it's 4 or less, you round down.

$$2.44 \longrightarrow 2.4$$

If there's a 9 in the tenths column, you may have to add one to the whole numbers.

$$2.97 \longrightarrow 3.0$$

Keep a 0 in the tenths column.

Round the decimals below, then find your answers in the picture below to reveal something that's for sale in the museum shop.

Round these to the nearest whole number:

5.6 →
7.2 →
9.9 →
4.3 →
4.9 →

...and fill them in green.

Round these to the nearest tenth:

4.45 →
0.95 →
3.64 →
9.82 →
7.44 →

...and fill them in red.

(Leave all the other numbers blank.)

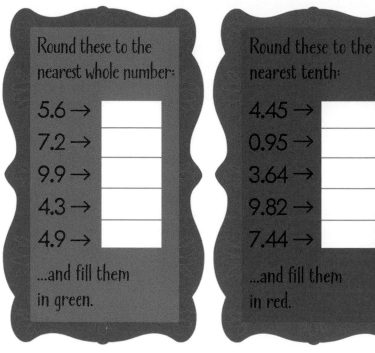

40

Find price labels from the sticker pages for the items in the museum shop.
Then use the clues below to figure out where each price label goes.

ACTIVITY BOOK

The Ancient Egyptian mask cost £10.50, but it's half price today.

The Roman helmet costs £1.40 more than the toy dinosaur.

The globe used to be £10.00, but now it's £2.60 less.

If you bought the activity book with £10.00, you'd get £3.40 change.

Fill this display case using stickers – making sure you match the amounts on the stickers to the answers.

1.2 + 1.2	0.8 + 0.9
1.9 − 0.4	1.9 + 2.0
8.2 − 1.6	2.1 + 1.9

How much would it cost to buy all four souvenirs, to the nearest pound?

£2.59   £0.55   £1.20   £3.45

Use this space for working out.

TOTAL

41

Write these fractions as decimals.

$$\frac{7}{10} =$$

$$\frac{3}{4} =$$

$$\frac{57}{100} =$$

$$\frac{2}{5} =$$

Write these decimals as fractions over 10 or 100.

0.4 =

0.55 =

0.8 =

0.09 =

Score

8

Sticker

Find the answers to these addition and subtraction questions.

2.1+0.4=

8.2−2.8=

0.65−0.3=

£2.50+£3.20=

$1.20−$0.90=

0.5+1.05=

Score

6

Sticker

42

Figure out the value of these decimal questions.

0.9 of 20 =

0.25 of 12 =

0.5 of 30 =

0.75 of 16 =

0.2 of 20 =

0.3 of 100 =

Score	Sticker
6	☆

Round these decimals to the nearest whole number.

5.05 ⟶

1.49 ⟶

2.75 ⟶

8.09 ⟶

Round these decimals to the nearest tenth.

8.34 ⟶

0.37 ⟶

0.89 ⟶

1.99 ⟶

Score	Sticker
8	☆

Percentages

Percentages are another way of writing fractions out of 100. The sign % stands for 'percent' which means 'out of 100'.

Can you fill in the gaps?

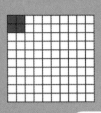 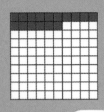   

$$\frac{4}{100} = \boxed{4\%} \qquad \frac{16}{100} = \boxed{16\%} \qquad \frac{22}{100} = \boxed{} \qquad \frac{60}{100} = \boxed{}$$

You don't actually have to have 100 things. Whatever you begin with counts as 100%. You can find a percentage of a shape...

100% 75% 50% 25%

...or a percentage of any number.

If 100% = 8   then   75% = 6   50% = $\boxed{}$ 25% = $\boxed{}$

The *actual* value of a percentage depends on how much you had to start with.

For example, 50% of 6 bricks is 3...

...but 50% of 16 bricks is 8.

If there were 100 bricks, 50% would be 50.

Fractions, decimals and percentages

To turn a fraction into a percentage, convert the fraction into hundredths first.

3 out of 4 builders have cheese sandwiches for lunch. What percentage is that?

$$\frac{3}{4} \overset{\times 25}{\underset{\times 25}{=}} \frac{75}{100} = 75\%$$

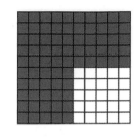

To convert a percentage into a fraction, write the percentage as a fraction over 100, then simplify it.

25% of people on the building site like peanut butter sandwiches. What's that as a fraction?

$$25\% = \frac{25}{100} \overset{\div 25}{\underset{\div 25}{=}} \frac{1}{4}$$

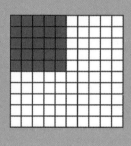

To convert a decimal into a percentage, multiply it by 100.

These pipes are 0.5 copper and 0.5 brass. What's that as a percentage?

$$0.5 \times 100 = 50\%$$

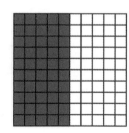

To convert a percentage into a decimal, you do the opposite: *divide* by 100.

20% of our hard hats are red. What's that as a decimal?

$$20 \div 100 = 0.2$$

Just like fractions and decimals, you can put percentages on a number line to show their size.

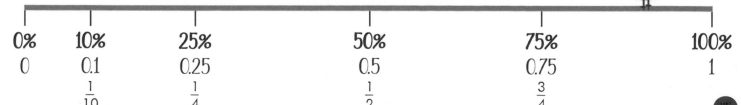

0%	10%	25%	50%	75%	100%
0	0.1	0.25	0.5	0.75	1
	$\frac{1}{10}$	$\frac{1}{4}$	$\frac{1}{2}$	$\frac{3}{4}$	

Converting percentages

Here are the most common conversions.
It's helpful to remember these.

$\frac{1}{10} \rightarrow 0.1 \rightarrow 10\%$

$\frac{1}{2} \rightarrow 0.5 \rightarrow 50\%$

$\frac{1}{4} \rightarrow 0.25 \rightarrow 25\%$

$\frac{3}{4} \rightarrow 0.75 \rightarrow 75\%$

$\frac{1}{5} \rightarrow 0.2 \rightarrow 20\%$

300 Red Rovers fans and 100 Blues United fans are watching the game. What percentage of the total support each team?

.... %   .... %

Can you convert these statistics into percentages?

I've saved 7 out of 10 goal attempts.

.... % saved

I've scored 5 goals, and 2 were headers.

.... % headers

We've played half of our matches at home.

.... % home games

We've played 4 matches this season, and won 3.

.... % wins

Can you help the commentators work out how many goals each team has scored?

Blues United have made 12 shots at goal. 25% of them went in.

Red Rovers have only made 10 shots at goal, but 30% went in.

Blues United scored .... goals.

Red Rovers scored .... goals.

Fill in the percentages in the league table. The team with the highest percentage of wins will be top of the league. Put a sticker trophy next to its name.

	Games	Wins	% wins
Town Tigers	10	3	
City Cubs	5	2	
Red Rovers	20	5	
Soccer Union	12	9	
Blues United	10	6	

If you have a club membership, which club's tickets are cheaper?

....is cheaper.

BLUES UNITED

Single ticket – £30.00

Members' discount – 50% off

RED ROVERS

Single ticket – £40.00

Members' discount – 75% off

Finding percentages

To find a percentage of a number, you can divide the number by 100, and then multiply the result by the percentage.

What's 30% of 50?

$$50 \div 100 = 0.5$$

$$0.5 \times 30 = 15$$

But often, there's a quicker way to do it.

What's 60% of 120?

60% is 50% plus 10% – which are easier to work out separately.

$$50\% \text{ (a half) of } 120 = 60$$

$$10\% \text{ (a tenth) of } 120 = 12$$

Add them together to get the answer: 72.

What's 30% of 150?

150 is 100 plus 50.

$$30\% \text{ of } 100 = 30$$

30% of 50 will be half of your *first* answer...

$$30\% \text{ of } 50 = 15$$

Add them together to get the answer: 45.

Here's a journal from a dinosaur dig.
Can you answer the questions?

We found 140 bones today. 25% of them were from a diplodocus skeleton. How many is that?

(Hint: 25% is a quarter, so halve and halve again.)

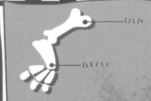

We found 45 enormous leg bones. 20% were from a T-Rex. How many is that?

(Hint: Find 10%, then multiply your answer by 2.)

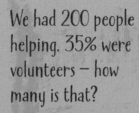

We had 200 people helping. 35% were volunteers – how many is that?

(Hint: Find 35% of 100, then multiply by 2.)

Can you find a route to the dinosaur skeleton? Answer each question, and follow the correct answer on to the next question to find a route that doesn't disturb the dig.

Start here.
5% of 80

90% of 110

70% of 150

15% of 60

20% of 25

75% of 12

25% of 40

10% of 70

3% of 200

50% of 36

75% of 12

4, 99, 8, 90, 105, 10, 110, 5, 20, 9, 7, 9, 15, 9, 8, 10, 18, 6, 16, 9, 10

The red cable cars have 12 seats, and the blue cable cars have 10 seats.

This car is 75% full. How many people are inside?

6 of the seats in here are full. What's that as a percentage of the total?

%

Only 3 of the seats are taken. What percentage is free?

%

There are 3 free seats in here. What percentage of the total seats is that?

%

SKI SHOP

You can use the roof for your working, if you like.

There's a sale on at the ski shop. Can you write in the new prices?

20% OFF

Jacket was $20.00

Now

$

Boots were $30.00

Now

$

Skis were $15.00

Now

$

Gloves were $10.00

Now

$

There are 120 pupils at the ski school. 20% of them are beginners – how many is that?

25% of the pupils fell over – how many is that?

15% of the pupils skied down the steepest slope. How many is that?

Ski School

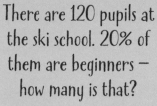

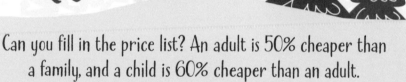

Can you fill in the price list? An adult is 50% cheaper than a family, and a child is 60% cheaper than an adult.

This survey asked 500 people which sport they liked best. Can you turn the results into percentages?

SKI PASSES

PRICES	
Family	£10.00
Adult	£
Child	£

	Number of people	%
Snowboarding	200	
Skiing	250	
Tobogganing	50	

Remember, your answers should add up to 100%.

Convert these fractions and decimals into percentages.

$0.08 =$

$\dfrac{3}{4} =$

$0.35 =$

$\dfrac{1}{5} =$

$\dfrac{16}{20} =$

Convert these percentages into decimals.

$66\% =$

$3\% =$

$30\% =$

Score $\dfrac{}{8}$

Sticker

Work out the value of these percentages.

50% of $26 =$

20% of $15 =$

15% of $40 =$

30% of $150 =$

80% of $30 =$

75% of $60 =$

Score $\dfrac{}{6}$

Sticker

Work out the new prices.

What's £2.00 with 10% off?

What's €5.00 with 50% off?

What's £4.00 with 20% off?

What's $11.00 with 10% off?

What's €40.00 with 25% off?

Circle the biggest one in each pair.

50% of 30 $\frac{7}{10}$ of 20

25% of 40 $\frac{2}{3}$ of 30

80% of 100 $\frac{8}{9}$ of 99

10% of 40 $\frac{1}{3}$ of 15

20% of 15 $\frac{1}{8}$ of 16

Score   Sticker

___
5

Score   Sticker

___
5

53

Help the aquarium keep track of the creatures in this tank, and simplify your answers.

Of the sharks, what fraction has stripes?

Of the starfish, what fraction is red?

Of the sea horses, what fraction is green?

Of the turtles, what fraction has spots?

The aquarium shop is having a sale. Can you work out the new prices of these toys?

40% off!

WAS €10.00
NOW

20% off!

WAS €15.00
NOW

50% off!

WAS €9.00
NOW

Fill these tanks with fish from the sticker pages. Add as many as you like, as long as they fit the clues.

Half of the fish in this tank are green.

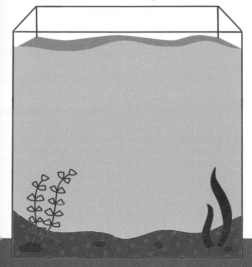

Three quarters of the fish in this tank are blue.

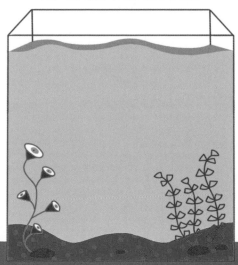

Three fifths of the fish in this tank are red.

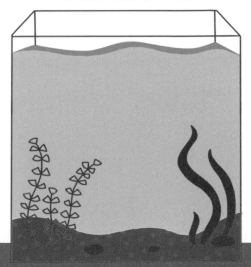

These guides asked visitors what they liked best at the aquarium. Can you work out their results as percentages?

I asked 100 visitors and 60 liked lobsters the best.

I asked 80 visitors and 20 of them preferred the giant squid.

80 out of the 160 visitors I asked liked the sharks the best.

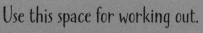

Use this space for working out.

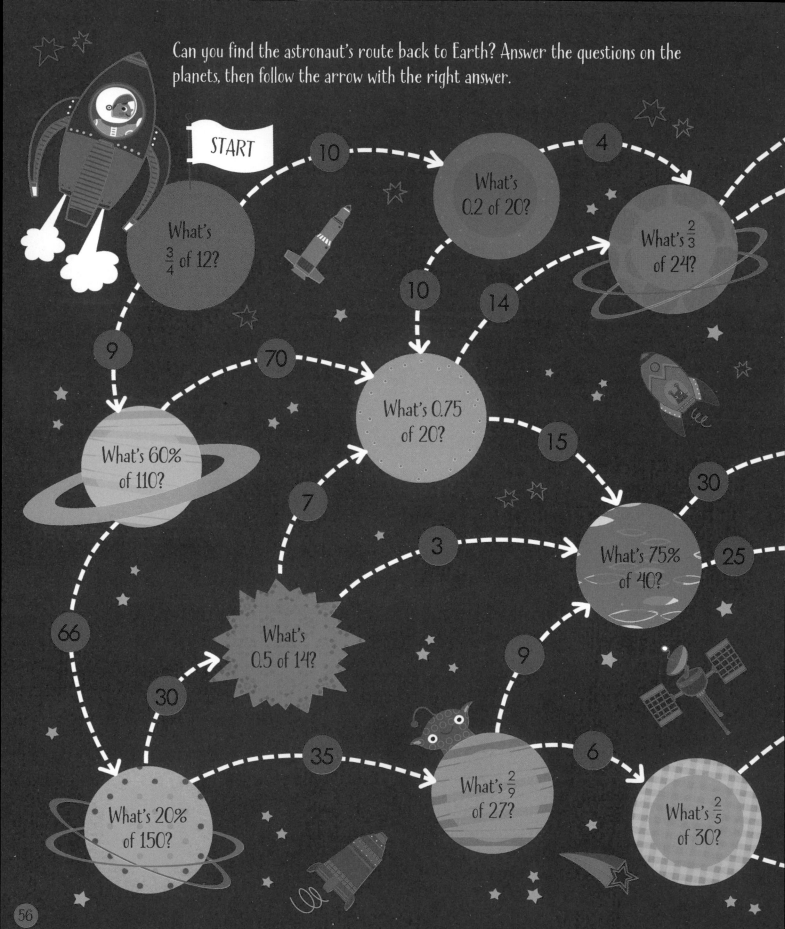

Can you find the astronaut's route back to Earth? Answer the questions on the planets, then follow the arrow with the right answer.

START

10

4

What's $\frac{3}{4}$ of 12?

What's 0.2 of 20?

What's $\frac{2}{3}$ of 24?

9

70

10

14

What's 0.75 of 20?

15

30

What's 60% of 110?

7

3

What's 75% of 40?

25

66

9

What's 0.5 of 14?

30

35

6

What's 20% of 150?

What's $\frac{2}{9}$ of 27?

What's $\frac{2}{5}$ of 30?

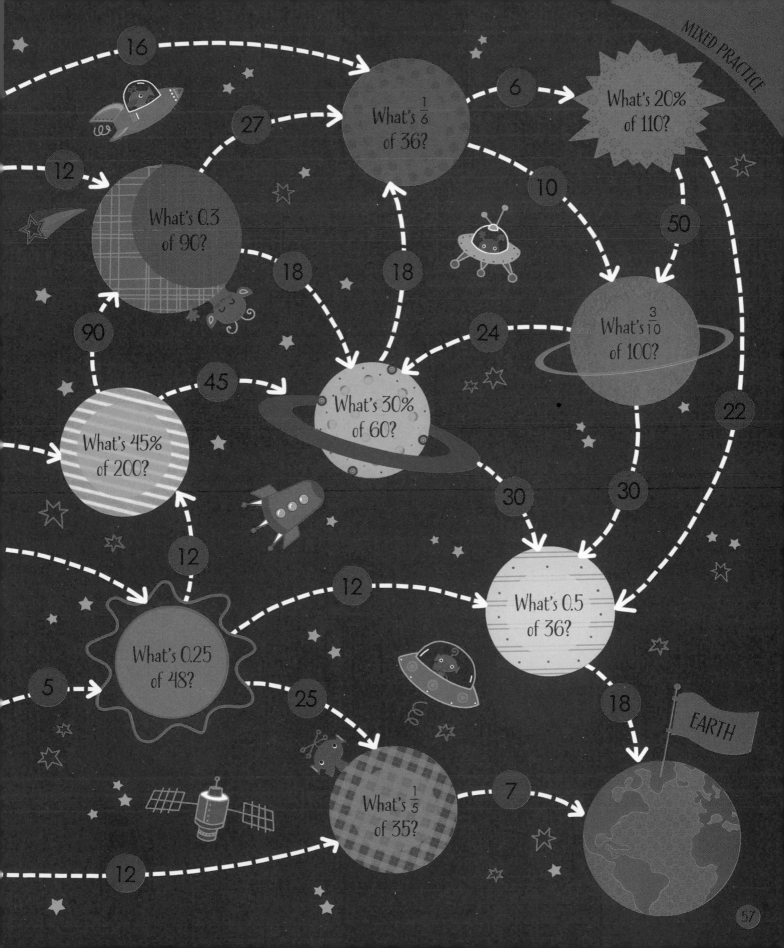

16

6

What's 20% of 110?

What's $\frac{1}{6}$ of 36?

27

12

What's 0.3 of 90?

10

50

18

18

What's $\frac{3}{10}$ of 100?

90

24

45

What's 30% of 60?

22

What's 45% of 200?

12

30

30

12

What's 0.5 of 36?

What's 0.25 of 48?

5

25

18

EARTH

What's $\frac{1}{5}$ of 35?

7

12

Answers
4-5 Halves, thirds and quarters

This mouse has eaten a half.

This mouse has eaten a quarter.

From left to right, the mice have eaten $\frac{1}{2}$, $\frac{1}{4}$ and $\frac{1}{3}$.

The brown mouse eats 2 chunks of cheese. The white mouse eats 2 chunks of cheese.

There should be 6 brown mice, 4 black mice and 2 white mice.

The white mouse is hungrier.

6-7 How many shares?

The customers at the table will get $\frac{2}{3}$ of an ice cream each.

$\frac{2}{10}$ of the sundaes have sprinkles.

$\frac{3}{10}$ of the sundaes have pink ice cream.

$\frac{1}{10}$ of the sundaes have orange ice cream.

$\frac{5}{10}$ of the sundaes have strawberries.

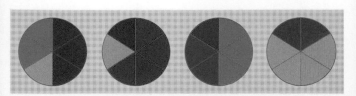

8-9 Equivalent fractions

From left to right, the squirrel's acorns are:

These fractions aren't equivalent to the others.

From left to right: 2 eggs have spots, 2 eggs have spots, 6 eggs have spots and 4 eggs have spots.

The baby bird's nest has $\frac{3}{8}$ on it.

10-11 Simplifying fractions

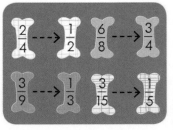

$\frac{6}{13}$ and $\frac{4}{7}$ can't be simplified any further.

$\frac{4}{6}$ or $\frac{2}{3}$ of the dogs have a collar.

$\frac{2}{4}$ or $\frac{1}{2}$ of the collars are pink.

$\frac{3}{6}$ or $\frac{1}{2}$ of the dogs have bows.

$\frac{6}{9}$ or $\frac{2}{3}$ of the bows are yellow.

First place: SOCKS
Second place: ALFIE
Third place: FLICK

12–13 Proper, improper and mixed fractions

The knight with $\frac{15}{5}$ defeated the dragon.

Yes, there are enough pies. (They want $3\frac{2}{3}$ in total.)

14–15 Using fractions to divide

There should be 3 stickers on each plate. $\frac{3}{4}$ of a whole cake is on each plate.

The answers to the pizza puzzle are: $\frac{2}{3}$ of a pineapple pizza, $\frac{4}{7}$ of a pepperoni pizza and $\frac{5}{6}$ of a mushroom pizza.

There will be $\frac{2}{3}$ of a bottle of apple juice in each cup, $\frac{1}{2}$ of a carton of popcorn in each bowl, and $\frac{1}{2}$ of a slice of melon on each plate.

From left to right, the balloons are: $2\frac{1}{2}$, $\frac{2}{3}$, $1\frac{3}{5}$, $\frac{1}{2}$, $\frac{1}{3}$, $\frac{2}{5}$ and $3\frac{1}{3}$.

16–17 Finding a fraction of a number

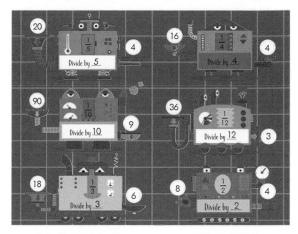

From left to right, the robots delivered 3 boxes, 5 boxes, 9 boxes (this one gets the sticker) and 5 boxes.

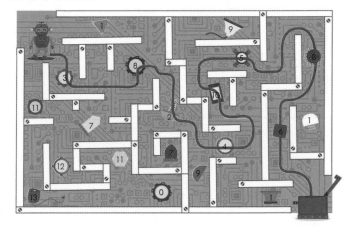

18–19 Finding more fractions

$\frac{3}{10}$ of 60 is 18.

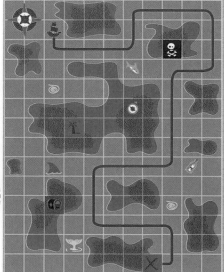

This box contains the most treasure.

20–21 Comparing fractions

The scarves ($\frac{12}{15}$ off) are a better deal than the T-shirts ($\frac{10}{15}$ off).

The dresses ($\frac{8}{14}$ off) are a better deal than the bags ($\frac{7}{14}$ off).

The watch stand has sold the biggest fraction ($\frac{15}{20}$ compared to $\frac{12}{20}$).

From left to right the shoppers' bags have zigzags, flowers, spots and stripes.

22–23 Adding and subtracting fractions

In total, the goat and her kid eat $\frac{5}{6}$ of the food.

From left to right, the stables have a brown horse, a black horse and a white horse.

The sum of all the fractions on the sheep is 3.

In total, the chickens, chicks and roosters eat $2\frac{7}{8}$ bags of seed.

24–25 More practice

From left to right, the monkeys have: $\frac{1}{3}$, $\frac{2}{3}$ and $\frac{1}{2}$.

You should add 4 green frogs and 3 red frogs to the leaves.

Each toucan gets $2\frac{2}{3}$ mangos.

From left to right, the butterflies' numbers are 15, 12, 6, 8, 3 and 9. The page should look like this:

The orange snake has 2 yellow sections and 4 blue sections.

The pink snake has 2 purple sections, 5 green sections and 1 yellow section.

The blue snake has 3 yellow sections, 2 red sections and 4 green sections.

26–27 Quick Quizzes

 $\frac{2}{3}$ $\frac{3}{8}$ $\frac{3}{12} = \frac{1}{4}$

 $\frac{7}{10}$ $\frac{2}{5}$ $\frac{4}{10} = \frac{2}{5}$

$\frac{3}{4}$ $\frac{5}{8}$ $\frac{3}{6} = \frac{1}{2}$

 $\frac{5}{6}$ $\frac{1}{7}$ $\frac{14}{20} = \frac{7}{10}$

$\frac{7}{4} = 1\frac{3}{4}$

$\frac{10}{3} = 3\frac{1}{3}$

$\frac{17}{8} = 2\frac{1}{8}$

$\frac{2}{3}$ of 15 = 10

$\frac{3}{4}$ of 12 = 9

$\frac{3}{10}$ of 30 = 9

$\frac{4}{7}$ of 21 = 12

$\frac{5}{6}$ of 18 = 15

$\frac{1}{4}$ of 20 = 5

$\frac{2}{3} + \frac{2}{3} = 1\frac{1}{3}$

$\frac{1}{3} - \frac{1}{6} = \frac{1}{6}$

$\frac{4}{5} - \frac{3}{10} = \frac{1}{2}$

$\frac{1}{12} + \frac{2}{6} = \frac{5}{12}$

$\frac{3}{5} + \frac{2}{10} = \frac{4}{5}$

$\frac{1}{3} - \frac{1}{4} = \frac{1}{12}$

28–29 Decimals

$\frac{7}{10} = 0.7$ $\frac{2}{100} = 0.02$ $\frac{6}{1000} = 0.006$

From left to right, the numbers on the number line are: 7.5, 10.3, 11.7 and 13.3.

30–31 Tenths and hundredths

The answers in the box on the left-hand page, from left to right, are: 0.8, 2.3 and 7.7.

$\frac{3}{10}$ or 0.3 of the cars are red.

$\frac{6}{10}$ or 0.6 of the cars have open tops.

$\frac{2}{10}$ or 0.2 of the cars are blue.

The empty space is 0.2.

The answers in the box on the right-hand page, from left to right, are: 0.04 and 0.36.

32–33 Metric measurements

From top to bottom the sweets are 6.6 cm, 6.2 cm and 6.5 cm.

The customer should buy the 1.2 kg bag of flour.

34–35 Decimal money

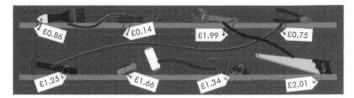

Everything will cost €20.00, so the customer won't get any change.

The lampshade cost £6.50. The mop cost $5.60. The planks cost €10.20.

The saw is now $2.25. The spade is now $1.60. The toolbox is now $2.50.

The customers will pay £2.50 for the pink paint, £3.00 for the blackboard paint and £2.40 for the glow in the dark paint.

36–37 More conversions

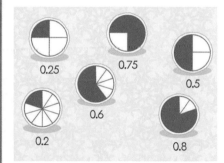

You should add the fish with these decimals: 0.25, 0.8, 0.2 and 0.5.

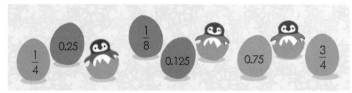

The giant squid has 4 tentacles with yellow spots, 2 tentacles with pink spots and 2 tentacles with green spots.

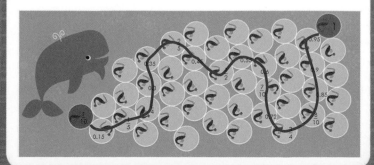

38–39 Finding a decimal of a number

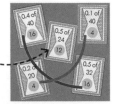

0.1 of 10	0.3 of 50	0.7 of 20	0.5 of 20
1	15	14 WINNER	10

This is the winning card.

The darts have won 20 points altogether.

2 balls go in the left basket and 3 balls go in the right basket.

He hits all 4 bumper cars.

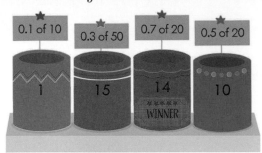

40–41 Rounding decimals

The numbers rounded to the nearest whole number are 6, 7, 10, 4 and 5.

The numbers rounded to the nearest tenth are: 4.5, 1.0, 3.6, 9.8 and 7.4.

£7.40

£5.70

ACTIVITY BOOK £6.60

£5.25

£7.10

2.4	1.7
1.5	3.9
6.6	4

All four souvenirs would cost £8.00, to the nearest pound.

42–43 Quick Quizzes

$\frac{7}{10} = 0.7$

$\frac{3}{4} = 0.75$

$\frac{57}{100} = 0.57$

$\frac{2}{5} = 0.4$

$0.4 = \frac{4}{10}$

$0.55 = \frac{55}{100}$

$0.8 = \frac{8}{10}$

$0.09 = \frac{9}{100}$

0.9 of 20 = 18
0.25 of 12 = 3
0.5 of 30 = 15
0.75 of 16 = 12
0.2 of 20 = 4
0.3 of 100 = 30

$2.1 + 0.4 = 2.5$
$8.2 - 2.8 = 5.4$
$0.65 - 0.3 = 0.35$
£2.50 + £3.20 = £5.70
$1.20 - $0.90 = $0.30
$0.5 + 1.05 = 1.55$

5.05 ---> 5
1.49 ---> 1
2.75 ---> 3
8.09 ---> 8
8.34 ---> 8.3
0.37 ---> 0.4
0.89 ---> 0.9
1.99 ---> 2.0

44–45 Percentages

The missing percentages are 22% and 60%.

50% of 8 = 4
25% of 8 = 2

46–47 Converting percentages

75% of the total support Red Rovers and 25% support Blues United.

The percentages are: 70% saved, 40% headers, 50% home games and 75% wins.

The league table should look like this:

	Games	Wins	% wins
Town Tigers	10	3	30%
City Cubs	5	2	40%
Red Rovers	20	5	25%
Soccer Union	12	9	75%
Blues United	10	6	60%

Blues United and Red Rovers both scored 3 goals.

Soccer Union are top of the league.

With a members' discount, Blues United tickets are £15.00 and Red Rovers are £10.00, so Red Rovers are cheaper.

48–49 Finding percentages

35 of the bones were from a diplodocus skeleton.

9 of the enormous leg bones were from a T-Rex.

70 of the people helping were volunteers.

50–51 More practice

From left to right, the answers on the cable cars are: 9, 60%, 75% and 30%.

The gloves are now $8.00. The jacket is now $16.00. The boots are now $24.00. The skis are now $12.00.

24 pupils are beginners. 30 pupils fell over. 18 pupils skied down the steepest slope.

An adult costs £5.00. A child costs £2.00.

40% liked snowboarding best, 50% liked skiing best and 10% liked tobogganing best.

52–53 Quick Quizzes

$0.08 = 8\%$	50% of 26 = 13
$\frac{3}{4} = 75\%$	20% of 15 = 3
	15% of 40 = 6
$0.35 = 35\%$	30% of 150 = 45
	80% of 30 = 24
$\frac{1}{5} = 20\%$	75% of 60 = 45
$\frac{16}{20} = 80\%$	
	£2.00 with 10% off = £1.80
$66\% = 0.66$	€5.00 with 50% off = €2.50
	£4.00 with 20% off = £3.20
$3\% = 0.03$	$11.00 with 10% off = $9.90
$30\% = 0.3$	€40.00 with 25% off = €30.00

50% of 30 (15) is bigger than $\frac{7}{10}$ of 20 (14).

$\frac{2}{3}$ of 30 (20) is bigger than 25% of 40 (10).

$\frac{8}{9}$ of 99 (88) is bigger than 80% of 100 (80).

$\frac{1}{3}$ of 15 (5) is bigger than 10% of 40 (4).

20% of 15 (3) is bigger than $\frac{1}{8}$ of 16 (2).

54–55 More practice

$\frac{1}{2}$ of the sharks have stripes.

$\frac{3}{5}$ of the starfish are orange.

$\frac{1}{4}$ of the sea horses are green.

$\frac{3}{4}$ of the turtles have spots.

The lobster toy is now €6.00.
The squid toy is now €12.00.
The shark toy is now €4.50.

You could have solved the fish tank puzzle like this:
3 green fish, 3 other fish
3 blue fish, 1 other fish
3 red fish, 2 other fish

60% of the visitors liked lobsters the best, 25% of visitors preferred the giant squid and 50% of visitors liked the sharks the best.

56–57 More practice

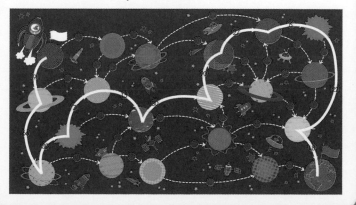

Fraction wall

This 'fraction wall' shows how the most common fractions compare.
You can use it to help you with the puzzles in this book.

Find equivalent fractions by looking for groups of bricks with the same width.

Use the fraction wall to compare the *sizes* of fractions.

As you go up the wall, the fractions get bigger.

As you go down, they get smaller.

1

| $\frac{1}{2}$ | $\frac{1}{2}$ |

| $\frac{1}{3}$ | $\frac{1}{3}$ | $\frac{1}{3}$ |

| $\frac{1}{4}$ | $\frac{1}{4}$ | $\frac{1}{4}$ | $\frac{1}{4}$ |

| $\frac{1}{5}$ | $\frac{1}{5}$ | $\frac{1}{5}$ | $\frac{1}{5}$ | $\frac{1}{5}$ |

| $\frac{1}{6}$ | $\frac{1}{6}$ | $\frac{1}{6}$ | $\frac{1}{6}$ | $\frac{1}{6}$ | $\frac{1}{6}$ |

| $\frac{1}{7}$ | $\frac{1}{7}$ | $\frac{1}{7}$ | $\frac{1}{7}$ | $\frac{1}{7}$ | $\frac{1}{7}$ | $\frac{1}{7}$ |

| $\frac{1}{8}$ | $\frac{1}{8}$ | $\frac{1}{8}$ | $\frac{1}{8}$ | $\frac{1}{8}$ | $\frac{1}{8}$ | $\frac{1}{8}$ | $\frac{1}{8}$ |

| $\frac{1}{9}$ | $\frac{1}{9}$ | $\frac{1}{9}$ | $\frac{1}{9}$ | $\frac{1}{9}$ | $\frac{1}{9}$ | $\frac{1}{9}$ | $\frac{1}{9}$ | $\frac{1}{9}$ |

| $\frac{1}{10}$ | $\frac{1}{10}$ | $\frac{1}{10}$ | $\frac{1}{10}$ | $\frac{1}{10}$ | $\frac{1}{10}$ | $\frac{1}{10}$ | $\frac{1}{10}$ | $\frac{1}{10}$ | $\frac{1}{10}$ |

| $\frac{1}{11}$ | $\frac{1}{11}$ | $\frac{1}{11}$ | $\frac{1}{11}$ | $\frac{1}{11}$ | $\frac{1}{11}$ | $\frac{1}{11}$ | $\frac{1}{11}$ | $\frac{1}{11}$ | $\frac{1}{11}$ | $\frac{1}{11}$ |

| $\frac{1}{12}$ | $\frac{1}{12}$ | $\frac{1}{12}$ | $\frac{1}{12}$ | $\frac{1}{12}$ | $\frac{1}{12}$ | $\frac{1}{12}$ | $\frac{1}{12}$ | $\frac{1}{12}$ | $\frac{1}{12}$ | $\frac{1}{12}$ | $\frac{1}{12}$ |

Edited by Rosie Dickins Managing designer: Zoe Wray Additional designs by Holly Lamont

First published in 2017 by Usborne Publishing Ltd., 83-85 Saffron Hill, London, EC1N 8RT, England. www.usborne.com Copyright © 2017 Usborne Publishing Ltd.

The name Usborne and the devices 🔮 ⊕ are Trade Marks of Usborne Publishing Ltd. All rights reserved. No part of this publication may be reproduced, stored in a retrieval system, or transmitted in any form or by any means, electronic, mechanical, photocopy, recording or otherwise, without prior permission of the publisher. UKE.

Finding a fraction of a number

Give this sticker to one of the robots on page 17.

Finding more fractions

Complete the pirate treasure map on page 19 using these stickers.

Add this goblet to a treasure chest on page 18.

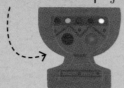

Adding and subtracting fractions

Put the horses in their stalls on page 22.

More practice

These frogs go on the leaves on page 24.

Add these butterflies to page 25.

Tenths and hundredths

Put these cars in the parking spaces on page 30.

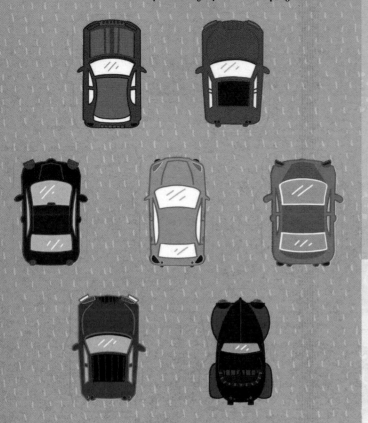

More conversions

Choose four of these fish for page 36.

These penguins have just hatched. Stick them down on page 37.

Finding a decimal of a number

This golden ticket goes on page 38.

Add these balls to the baskets on page 39.

More practice

Add these souvenirs to the display on page 41.

| 2.4 | 1.5 | 6.6 | 1.7 | 3.9 | 4 |

Add these price stickers to the souvenirs in the museum shop.

£7.40   £5.70   £6.60   £5.25   £7.10

Converting percentages

Award this cup to the team that is top of the league on page 47.

More practice

Use these fish to fill up the tanks at the aquarium on page 55.

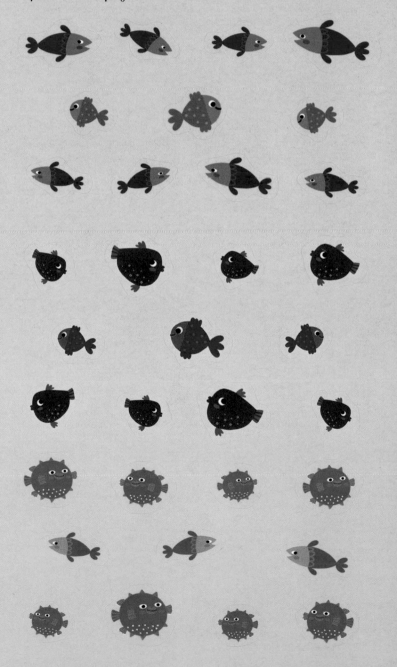

Quick Quizzes

Give yourself a star sticker each time you complete a Quick Quiz.